Walk on Holy Ground

RICKY CLEMONS

PUBLISHED BY FIEDLI PUBLISHING, INC.

Copyright ©2019, Ricky Clemons
ALL RIGHTS RESERVED.

No part of this publication may be reproduced, stored in a retrieval system, or transmitted in any form or by any means—electronic, mechanical, photo-copy, recording, or any other—except for brief quotation in reviews, without the prior permission of the author or publisher.

ISBN: 978-1-948638-40-1

Published by

Fideli Publishing, Inc.
119 W. Morgan St.
Martinsville, IN 46151
www.FideliPublishing.com

PRINTED IN THE UNITED STATES OF AMERICA

Table of Contents

God Can Handle Being God 1
God is Not Surprised 2
No Time Off 3
What is Truth? 4
Make-Believe 5
The Lord is About Giving Life 6
Life is Like a Mystery 7
Our Senses 8
No Matter 9
Shows Respect of Persons 10
Can't Love Us 12
It's So Easy to Get Absorbed Into 13
The Storms in Our Lives 14
Things Can Go Wrong 15
Salvation to Self 16
Life Can Be Like 17
The Lord Can Make Things Better for Us 18
We Can Misunderstand 19
You are Your Heart 20
It's a Blessing to 21
There is No Time Limit on God's Love for Us 22
On Top Of 23

Rise Up	24
So	25
There are a Lot of	26
Forget	27
In Our Minds	28
Nothing in This World	29
Jesus Uses Good Doctors and Good Nurses	30
Speaking the Truth	31
Is Like Heaven to a Lot of People	32
Everybody Can Believe	33
Need to Overcome	34
Being Around Nature	35
If You are Poor	36
Will Go Through Some Trials	37
How Much Longer Will it Be?	38
Some Educated People	39
The Joy of Life	40
We are Created in the Image of God	41
Some People	42
If We are Saved in Jesus	43
The Good Things that I Do	44
Like a Canoe Without Its Paddle	45
It's Like a Bad Dream	46
Some People Will Only Love You	47
The Devil Loves to Tempt Us	48

Is it Really Worth It?	49
We Can Bring Hardship on Ourselves	50
The Lord Will Bring	51
Put It Upon Our Hearts	52
We Are Living In	53
News Gets Around	54
In This Life	55
Some People Won't Like You	56
You Can Be Smart	57
Pass Over	58
Things Do Come Up	59
In This Present Day	60
What You Went Through	61
God is Forever Beyond	62
Have Bible Knowledge	63
Spreading the Gospel	64
What They Want to Hear	65
We Know That	66
A Quiet Night	67
A Double Life	68
The Deep Waters Of	69
No Matter What Good You Do	70
Everybody May Not	71
You and I Can Give Up on People	72
The Most Effective Ministry	73

When It's Usually Quiet	74
It's Done and Over With	75
We Will Very Often Remember	76
Who Can?	77
Only Jesus Can Help You Overcome	78
Jesus Lived a Normal Life	79
The Spiritual Things	80
I Know that I Will Be Blessed	81
Jesus Can Fix Broken People	82
When We Go Through	83
Is Ordinary	84
There are People	85
The Real True Life	86
You	88
God Created Us to Love	89
Everybody Will Answer to God	90
Do We Ever Trespass on God's Holy Ground?	91
Everybody Has a Sin Defect	92
My Soul Cries Out	93
Our Human Nature Knows	94
There are Many Brilliant People	95
The Truth Will Judge You	96
Who Are We?	97
You are Cleansing Me from my Sins	98
We Can Never Get Lost in Jesus	99
Can We Truly Accept?	100

Will Stand Still	101
Many People Believe in Themselves	102
When We Go to Heaven	103
Another Day	104
Knows Its Place	105
The Weather of Life	106
Someone Asked Me	107
Love is the Greatest Gift	108
The Lord is Still Working with Me	109
The Combination to Life	110
There is No Time in Eternity	111
The Lord's Yes and No	112
A Righteous Nation	113
God Loves Everybody	114
Motivate	115
Many People Believe	116
Being a Good Person	117
There are No Shortcuts in Life	118
Human Beings Will Usually	119
In the Books of History	120
There is No Former Life	121
What Will Jesus Write in the Dust?	122
In the Courtroom of Time	123

God Can Handle Being God

Lucifer was the most beautiful and most gifted angel up in heaven.

He couldn't handle that and was cast out of heaven with one third of the heavenly angels.

God can handle being God and that is why God is God.

Some people can't handle a job promotion. It will go to their heads.

Some people can't handle getting rich. It will go their heads.

Some people can't handle living in a brand-new house. It will go to their heads.

Some people can't handle driving a brand-new car. It will go to their heads.

God can handle being God.

No one can be more humble than God.

You and I can't always handle what God gives to us.

Our talents can go to our heads.

Our gifts can go to our heads.

Our ministries can go to our heads.

Our skills can go to our heads.

What we know can go to our heads.

God can handle being god to be worshipped and to be praised.

God is Not Surprised

God is not surprised about what we can do.

God created all human beings in his likeness.

It's up to us to use it.

We can be surprised to see a poor man getting rich.

One race of people can't keep another race of people in slavery forever. God won't allow it. The bible has proof of that.

God is in every race of people and wants them to prosper.

God is not surprised about who can be successful.

Every man, woman, boy and girl is the likeness of God.

God gives every race of people intelligence for greatness.

There are people who are surprised to see an uneducated person having good common sense.

God is not surprised.

God can make a simple man to be wise.

Every human being is created in the likeness of God, who can be surprised about nothing.

No Time Off

There is no time off from the Lord.

There is always something to do for the Lord.

There is no time off in living our life unto the Lord.

Living unto the Lord is twenty-four hours around the clock, every day.

Talking about the Lord has no time off for you and me.

We must always talk about the Lord when we get the opportunity to do so.

There is no time off from giving Jesus Christ, our Lord, all the glory and praise.

There is no time off for our minds to think on Jesus.

There is no time off for our hearts to love Jesus.

There is no time off from worshipping the Lord.

Our Lord and savior Jesus Christ doesn't take any time off from saving us from our sins.

Jesus doesn't take any time off from cleansing us from our sins.

There is no time off from confessing and repenting of our sins.

There is no time off from loving and obeying Jesus.

There is no time off from trusting the Lord Jesus Christ.

There is no time off from having a relationship with Jesus Christ.

The only time off that we have is when we die.

What is Truth?

What is truth that we should always believe?

What is truth that a righteous man, woman, boy and girl will speak?

What is truth that will sooner or later be revealed?

What is truth that a liar hates to speak?

What is truth that the devil hates?

What is truth that is Jesus Christ?

What is truth that is the holy spirit?

What is truth that is God?

What is truth that we should always live by?

What is truth that will set us free?

What is truth that is everlasting?

What is truth that cannot lie?

Is truth every word that we say?

Is truth everything that we do?

Is truth every thought that we think?

Is truth everything that we feel?

God always knows the truth.

Make-Believe

So many people love to watch make-believe movies.

The actors can pretend to possess God-like powers to move the viewers.

Make-believe things can surely get a lot of people's attention.

Some desire to believe that they have super powers to do anything they like.

Make-believe movies can lift us high up in pretense and can cause us to feel powerful.

Make-believe is not real, no matter how powerful it makes us feel.

Many people believe that God is make-believe.

They say that we Christians are weak and are a bunch of dreamers.

Many people believe that the bible is make-believe, like a fairy tale.

Many people believe that Christians' worshipping God is make-believe, because they can't See God.

Many people believe that we Christians make-believe that Jesus Christ is the son of God and the savior of the world.

Many people want to have God-like powers but don't believe that God exists.

There are church folks who will make-believe to do all things, but only God, the Father, the Son and God the holy spirit can do all things.

To make-believe is to not be real.

Reality is our limit that makes-believe will cross over.

The Lord is About Giving Life

Terrorists can kill more people than a hurricane.

Drugs can kill more people than an earthquake.

Diseases can kill more people than a war.

The Lord is about giving life in the land of the living.

A mass shooting can kill more people than a forest fire.

Wars can kill more people than an atomic bomb.

Genocides can kill more people than a tsunami.

The Lord is about giving life in the land of the living.

Abortions can kill more babies than natural disasters.

Serial killers can kill more people than tornadoes.

The Lord is about giving life in the land of the living.

Sin causes many people to kill many people.

The wages of sin is death.

The Lord Jesus Christ is about giving life.

Jesus is the life living in us.

Jesus created us to live and love especially Him the most day by day.

Life is Like a Mystery

Life is like a mystery, but we can't solve life.

Life can take us through some changes day after day.

Life will not give us a clue about what can come our way.

Life is like a mystery that changes its direction like the wind that blows.

We don't know where life will take us.

Life is visible but we can't see life's schedule for us.

Life can change its schedule on us any day.

Life is like a mystery that only Jesus Christ can solve.

We don't know life's motives and intentions, and they can catch us off guard.

We can sometimes see a trap and life can camouflage what is ahead of us.

Life is like a mystery because life is deep even in our sleep.

We can sleep away in life, and only Jesus can wake us up to see that life can betray us.

We can't predict life's path for us, but we can choose to live our lives unto Jesus Christ, because, to Him, life is no mystery.

Our Senses

Alcohol will dull our senses.

Eating too much food will dull our senses.

Not getting enough sleep will dull our senses.

Negative talking people will dull our senses.

Trying to get revenge will dull our senses.

Holding grudges will dull our senses.

Getting angry will dull our senses.

Not drinking enough water will dull our senses.

Working too much will dull our senses.

Not trusting the Lord will dull our senses.

Not doing the Lord's will dulls our senses.

Sinning against the Lord will dull our senses.

Turning our backs on the Lord will dull our senses.

Only the Lord Jesus Christ will surely sharpen our senses.

Loving and obeying Him and studying His holy word will sharpen our senses.

No Matter

No matter what the color of your skin, there are people who will ride on your bumper as if they will run you over.

No matter what gender you are, there are people who will judge you and me according to how they feel.

No matter where you live, there are people who won't like you no matter what good things you do.

No matter what good words you say, there are people who won't believe you day after day.

No matter how much you know, there are people who will know more things than you.

No matter who you are, there are people who will break your heart.

No matter whether you're rich or poor, there are people who will ignore you when you knock on their doors.

No matter how many sins you have committed, Jesus Christ will forgive you if you confess and repent and surrender your life unto Him.

Shows Respect of Persons

This world shows respect of persons.

The rich will get the most love.

The famous will get the most love.

Educated people will get the most love.

This world shows respect of persons.

Even in the church, the pastors and elders will get the most love.

The government leaders will get the most love.

Entertainers will get the most love.

Presidents and kings will get the most love.

Athletes will get the most love.

Homeless people won't get much love.

Disabled people won't get much love.

Mentally ill people won't get much love.

This world shows respect of persons.

Jesus Christ loves everybody all the same amount.

Jesus shows no favoritism to anyone.

This world shows favoritism even in the church.

Popular people will get the most love.

Attractive people will get the most love.

Successful people will get the most love.

This world shows respect of persons.

Jesus is not like this world.

Jesus Christ wants to save us all, great and small.

Criminals won't get much love.

People will pretty much accept that.

Jesus loves the criminals too, and he wants to save them from being lost.

Can't Love Us

Money cannot love us.

Money can get short and run out on us.

Food cannot love us. Food can cause us to become ill and overweight.

Clothes cannot love us. Clothes can wrinkle and fade.

Sex cannot love us. Sex can bring on a venereal disease from sleeping around.

A house cannot love us. A house can get old and need to be remodeled.

A vehicle cannot love us. A vehicle can break down on us and leave us helpless.

Time cannot love us. Time won't wait on us to wise up.

A job cannot love us. A job can cause us to overwork ourselves.

Material things cannot love us. Material things can get flooded with water and burn up in a fire.

Selfishness cannot love us. Selfishness can take away all the goodness in our hearts.

We can always be sure that Jesus Christ loves us.

He will supply all of our needs.

We could never love if Jesus had not died for our sins and risen from the grave.

It's So Easy to Get Absorbed Into

It's so easy to get absorbed into money.

It's so easy to get absorbed into food.

It's so easy to get absorbed into human beings.

It's so easy to get absorbed into your job.

It's so easy to get absorbed into your pets.

It's so easy to get absorbed into self.

It's so easy to get absorbed into your talents.

It's so easy to get absorbed into skills.

It's so easy to get absorbed into your house.

It's so easy to get absorbed into your church ministry.

It's so easy to get absorbed into your feelings.

It's so easy to get absorbed into the things in this world.

We need to get absorbed into Jesus Christ, who can cleanse us from our sins.

We need to get absorbed into Jesus Christ, who can save us from our sins.

Wee need to get absorbed into Jesus Christ, who is coming back again to absorb His righteous children into heaven.

The Storms in Our Lives

The storms in our lives can encourage us to pray more and more.

A storm can come in our life on any day.

The storms in our lives can help us to draw closer to Jesus Christ our Lord, who we can call on in the storm.

The storms in our lives can be a blessing to us.

The storms in our lives can teach us a good lesson to put our trust in the Lord to bring us through the storm.

A storm can rage in the church for you and me to take shelter in Jesus.

Some church folks are like a storm that rages their words of pride upon our hearts.

The storms in our lives can humble us down and give us the push that we need to stay on God's holy ground.

The storms are not always something bad.

They can help us to wise up and be glad that a storm woke us up spiritually so we can see the truth.

Things Can Go Wrong

Things can go wrong when we least expect to not think about what could go wrong.

Things can go wrong that we have to face up to twenty-four hours around the clock.

Things can go wrong like not seeing a sharp piece of metal in the road and driving over it with our foot being heavy on the petal.

Things can go wrong like getting bit by an insect while sleeping in our beds at night.

The bite may be mild or severe, according to what type of insect it was.

Things can go wrong at any time of the day and night, and we need to pray to Jesus Christ.

Things can go wrong that we have no control over.

The things that could go wrong can be so bold to kill us dead, if Jesus allows it.

Things can go so wrong for me and you, who can believe in Jesus and be saved no matter what goes wrong in our lives.

Jesus will embrace us beyond the things that can go wrong on any given day.

Salvation to Self

Salvation to self who must work out one's own soul salvation without a doubt.

Salvation to self who will choose to believe in Jesus Christ to be saved or will not choose to believe in Jesus Christ.

Salvation to self who will receive eternal life or not receive eternal life.

Salvation to self who will be saved or lost when Jesus comes back again.

Salvation to self who has sins to confess and repent of unto Jesus Christ, who has no end.

Salvation to self who has an end, if self is lost in the grave.

Salvation to self who should be thankful unto God, who gave us his only begotten son who self can be saved in.

Salvation to self who will walk down the road to destiny when Jesus is a friend to self who can choose heaven or hell.

Salvation to self will surely fail without the goodness of God leading self to repent.

Life Can Be Like

Life can be like the heat from the sun.

Life can get hot with many people doing the wrong things.

Life can be like the shade from the trees.

Life can cool us off with some peace that we need.

Life can be like a warm, gentle breeze.

Life can sooth our soul for us to believe that life can be good.

Life can be like the rain clouds in the sky.

Life can wet us up with disappointments, heartache and grief with no hard try.

Life can be like the grass on the ground.

Life will give us choices to make and we need to make Jesus Christ our choice.

Life can be like broken, dried up limbs if we are lost in our sin.

The Lord Can Make Things Better for Us

The Lord can make things better for us if we wait on Him.

It may take some years for the Lord to make things better for us.

It will be worth the wait to wait on the Lord Jesus Christ.

The Lord can make things better for us if we put our trust in Him.

We can always be sure about Jesus making things better for us.

If it's in his will to make things better for us in a day or week, it will happen.

The Lord can make things better for us if we love and obey Him.

The Lord loves to give a good life regardless of what we go through in our lives.

The Lord can relieve us of our heavy burdens on His time.

His strength lets us hold on to Him each and every day.

The Lord can make things better for us who don't have a clue how the Lord is working things out for us even when we lay down to sleep and don't know what is going on.

We can sleep away in our dreams when the Lord can make things better for us according to His will.

We Can Misunderstand

We can misunderstand what someone says that we can take the wrong way.

What someone says we may twist it up like a wet cloth and try to squeeze out some water.

The water that we squeeze out may be filthy with what we misunderstand.

We can misunderstand what someone does and we can take it the wrong way.

We might criticize that person and judge them.

Someone can say something good to sound so plain and simple.

Someone can do something good to be so plain and simple.

It's how we hear the words and how we see what someone does to understand or misunderstand him or her.

Jesus Christ, our Lord and savior, was misunderstood sometimes because some people took him in the wrong way.

They were really into themselves like wanting to be seen when they pray.

You are Your Heart

You are your heart by what you say, whether you say words of truth or lies, day after day.

You are your heart by what you think, whether they are thoughts of good or evil that the Lord always sees.

You are your heart by what you do for the right reasons or the wrong reasons that the Lord will bring into the light.

You are your heart to love or hate. This will sooner or later show and tell in your life so read.

You are your heart to choose with your free will choice. You can choose to do good or evil without any force.

You are your heart to love and obey Jesus Christ or to choose to live for the devil, who will destroy your life.

You are your heart to make your destiny to be heaven or hell.

Jesus is above your heart to set you free from condemning your heart to be saved in Him for your destiny to agree.

It's a Blessing to

It's a blessing to talk to our brothers and sisters in the Lord.

They can surely be good to talk to for as long as we live.

It's a blessing to know our brothers and sisters in the Lord.

They can surely be open about their sins and confess and repent of them unto the Lord Jesus Christ.

It's a blessing to be around our brothers and sisters in the Lord.

We all have one mind in Jesus Christ, and we are of one accord.

It's a blessing to love our brothers and sisters in the Lord.

We may not always understand one another but we can surely love one another.

It's a blessing to uplift and encourage our brothers and sisters in the Lord.

They are our church family and we pray together and get the power of the Holy Spirit to win souls unto the Lord.

There is No Time Limit on God's Love for Us

There is no time limit on God's love for us.

God's love is eternal love that goes on throughout every generation.

God's love for us is not only for this present day.

God's love was for the past days and now for the present and going into the future days.

There is no time limit on God's love for us.

He gave us His only begotten son, who is beyond time that is no time to Him.

There can be a time limit set on our love that takes time to grow much stronger.

There is a time that our love for one another can weaken if we don't spend some time with one another.

Our love for the Lord can weaken if we don't spend any time with Him.

There is no time limit for God's love that doesn't get weak on us.

God even loves those who are lost and gives them some time to repent and be saved.

There is no time limit on God's love for us.

God's love is all present when time can run out and not be seen when we need it.

There is no time limit on God's love for us.

His love will never end.

Our love can come to an end when we one day go to the grave.

On Top Of

The sky is on top of this world

The grass is on top of the ground.

The roof is on top of the house.

The rug is on top of the floor.

The mattress is on top of the box spring.

The stamp is on top of the envelope.

The sun is on top of the sky.

The stars are on top of outer space.

The tree is on top of its roots.

The head is on top of the body.

The clouds are on top of the mountain.

The mountain is on top of the valley.

The fence is on top of the grass.

The house is on top of the foundation.

The Christian is on top of the old cardinal mind.

The church is on top of sinners.

Jesus Christ is on top of the church.

Rise Up

Smoke will rise up in the sky and may not always have a bad odor.

The heart can rise up in wickedness to give life a bad odor.

Lava can rise up out of a volcano and melt anything in its way.

Bad thoughts can rise up out of the mind for anyone to say some bad words.

Steam can rise up out of the ground.

Selfishness can rise up on God's holy ground.

Boiling water can rise up out of a pot.

Our motives can rise up in our hearts for only God to cool off.

Pride can rise up in anyone's heart.

The Lord can humble it down to never rise up again.

No one can rise themselves up out of their sleep, if the Lord doesn't wake them up.

A man and woman and a boy and girl can rise up in riches and wealth.

If the Lord says that it's your time to lick the dust, death will take away your breath.

The sun will rise up in the early morning.

The Lord can rise up a child to love and obey Him in the early morning of his life.

Many adults love to rise up in greed and fame.

The humble saints will rise up in the book of life that has our names in it.

So

The grass will cover the ground so secure.

The trees will stand up on its roots so bold.

The flowers will bloom so beautiful.

The bees will buzz so sure.

The air will move so kind.

The clouds will sit up in the sky so peaceful.

The sky will cover the earth so sane.

The sun will shine so bright.

The moon will glow so mystic.

The day will be so eager to keep us awake.

The night will be so ready to let us sleep.

You and I will be so destined.

Jesus Christ, our Lord, will be so happy when he comes back again to take all of His children to heaven.

All the saints will be so happy to see Jesus one day soon.

There are a Lot of

There are a lot of good people in this world, regardless of the jailhouses.

There are a lot of good neighborhoods to live in, regardless of the bad neighborhoods.

There is a lot of justice in this world, regardless of the injustice.

There are a lot of good medicines that people can take, regardless of the bad medicine.

There are a lot of healthy people in this world, regardless of the bad health.

There are a lot of children in this world, regardless of many miscarriages.

There is a lot of love in this world, regardless of the hate.

There is a lot of peace in this world, regardless of the wars.

There are a lot of foods in this world, regardless of the starvation.

There are a lot of sane people in this world, regardless of the insanity.

There are a lot of intelligent people in this world, regardless of the stupidity.

There are a lot of wise people in this world, regardless of the foolishness.

There are a lot of houses in this world, regardless of the homeless.

There are a lot of Christians in this world, regardless of the wicked.

There are a lot of churches in this world, regardless \of some people having no spiritual life.

There are a lot of bibles in this world, regardless of people not reading them.

Forget

We can forget to say something that may help someone else.

We can forget to do something that we need to do.

We don't have a perfect memory to remember everything.

We were all born in sin that causes us to not remember everything.

There are many people who have a great memory to pass their college exams with all A's.

There are many people who have a great memory on their jobs and perform very well.

There are many church folks who have a great memory to remember many bible scriptures.

Only Jesus has a perfect memory.

He remembers every word that we say, whether they are good words or bad words.

He remembers everything that we do, whether they are good things or bad things.

We may not remember something that may cause us to lose our lives.

That's how bad our memories can sometimes be.

There are some things that we need to forget to move on in life.

Jesus Christ, our Lord and savior, will forget all of our sins if we confess and repent them unto Him.

We are so blessed that Jesus will do that for us.

In Our Minds

We can go to many places in our minds, like we're travel agents all the time.

We can think on many things day after day, and let our minds take us to many places.

If we keep Jesus Christ on our minds, He will take us to heavenly places in our minds where we can get lost for God's word to find us and set us free with the truth.

We can stay in the same place in our minds, like a root down in the ground.

We can take ourselves to many places in our minds, but Jesus will always know where we are.

We can go to many places in our minds that don't have any vacation spots, but without Jesus being in our minds from the start of the day to the end of the day, we are lost.

Nothing in This World

Nothing in this world is worth loving more than loving Jesus Christ, the Lord.

Nothing in this world is worth putting anything above the Lord Jesus Christ.

Nothing in this world is worth trusting more than trusting Jesus.

Nothing in this world is worth believing in more than believing in Jesus.

Nothing in this world is worth saving more than being saved in Jesus.

Nothing in this world is worth following more than following Jesus.

Nothing in this world is worth keeping more than keeping Jesus in your heart.

Nothing in this world is worth living for more than living for Jesus.

Nothing in this world is worth dying for more than dying for Jesus' name's sake.

Nothing in this world is worth keeping our minds on more than keeping our minds on Jesus.

Nothing in this world is worth talking about more than talking about Jesus.

Nothing in this world is worth dreaming about more than dreaming about Jesus Christ coming back one day soon to take us to heaven if we are saved in Him.

Jesus Uses Good Doctors and Good Nurses

A lot of criminals will act like they are mentally ill, but they have enough sanity to get in a car and drive up and down the dangerous highways.

If someone is truly mentally ill, he or she can't function normally to talk with good sense and to stay focused on doing something right, day after day.

People who are truly mentally ill will not be able to socialize with normal people.

Many mentally ill people are taking medications to help them to live a normal life, day after day.

There is no sanity in being insane.

An insane person can't live a normal life and live in a normal society.

No one has ever seen a mentally ill animal.

Only human beings can get a mental illness.

We are the most intelligent creatures on earth.

We were created in the image of God, and we have fallen down so low in our mental state of mind.

Many human beings have lost their minds and act worse than a wild animal.

It's so amazing how the mind can be restored to sanity through good medicine that the Lord has allowed to heal the mind.

Illnesses and diseases come from sin that is passed down from one generation to the next.

When Jesus Christ was here on earth, He healed many sick people and made them well as if they were never sick.

Jesus uses good doctors and good nurses to heal many sick people.

Speaking the Truth

One day in the afternoon, I was in a convenience store, standing in line to pay for what I had in my hand.

Before I left the store, I was standing in the checkout line and a man stepped in front of me to pay for what he had in his hand.

Time stood still.

I said to the man, "I was in front of you," and he told me to go ahead.

I looked at him and he looked at me as we stood there frozen in our footsteps.

I knew that I was in line ahead of him and he knew it too.

I don't think that I sinned against the Lord when I spoke the truth to that man.

I was not angry with him for getting in front of me.

I am glad he didn't have a hot temper.

I could have stood there and said nothing at all, but I chose to speak the truth.

The man accepted the truth in front of me and the other people in the store.

I thank the Lord that there was some good in him to let me check out before him.

Speaking the truth has got many people killed.

Speaking the truth can cause me and you to have many enemies who will get revenge at us for speaking the truth that they hate.

Jesus has always spoken the truth, even though he made many enemies who didn't accept the truth that is Jesus Christ.

Speaking the truth, especially in love, can surely change someone's life for the better.

Is Like Heaven to a Lot of People

Having a good paying job is like heaven to a lot of people.

Having a big beautiful house is like heaven to a lot of people.

Having a beautiful, expensive car is like heaven to a lot of people.

Having a college degree is like heaven to a lot of people.

Having a beautiful wife is like heaven to a lot of people.

Having a rich husband is like heaven to a lot of people.

Having very talented children is like heaven to a lot of people.

Having a lot of money is like heaven to a lot of people.

Having good health is like heaven to a lot of people.

Having a green card is like heaven to a lot of people.

There is only one true heaven.

That is the heaven that Jesus Christ, our Lord, will take us to for being saved in Him.

Jesus' heaven is eternal beyond this world that will one day pass away with the temporary heavens.

Everybody Can Believe

Everybody can believe that they are right about what they say.

Everybody can believe that it must be true about what they say.

What we say comes out of our hearts, whether we are right or wrong about what we say.

Only Jesus knows if we are always right about what we say.

We can say something and believe that we are right when we may be so wrong.

Everybody can believe that what they do must be the right thing to do, whether it's good or bad.

God's holy word will always let everybody know the right words to say and the right things to do.

We, especially the children of God, can believe that we are always right about what we say and do.

We know a lot of bible truth and may try to make someone look stupid if they don't speak the truth the way we know it.

Everybody can believe in Jesus Christ, even though everybody will not be on the same spiritual level.

Jesus understands everybody's spiritual level and knows people will use that to be right with Him.

Need to Overcome

Everybody in the church has some things in their life that they need to overcome.

Some church folks need to overcome their tongue from talking too much.

Some church folks need to overcome their appetites.

They eat too much food.

Some church folks need to overcome lust.

They lust with their eyes.

Some church folks need to overcome their pride.

They think highly of themselves.

Some church folks need to overcome money.

They love money too much.

Some church folks need to overcome material things.

Jesus can help us church folks overcome anything in our lives.

Jesus had to overcome all of our sins.

Being Around Nature

Being around nature will help us to think right.

Being around nature will give us some peace of mind.

Being around nature will help us to see things so clear.

Being around nature will help us to be in tune with what is real.

Being around nature will help us to see what is true.

Being around nature will help us to see what is in our hearts.

Being around nature will help us to sharpen our senses.

There were times when Jesus Christ, our Lord, was around nature when he went out to pray.

Jesus went up on the mountain to pray.

The Holy Spirit led Jesus out in the wilderness to fast for forty days and nights.

He was tempted by the devil and never sinned against God.

Being around nature is where God also dwells.

If You are Poor

If you are poor, hardly anyone will want to hang around you.

If you are poor, some of your kinfolks might not have anything to do with you.

If you are poor, you will have some neighbors who will despise you.

If you are poor, very often many people won't like you.

If you are poor, some people in the church won't want to be your friend.

If you are poor, some people in the church will believe that they are better than you.

Jesus Christ chose to be poor to save souls so they can be in the eternal kingdom of everlasting wealth.

Will Go Through Some Trials

Every Christian will go through some trials for Jesus' name's sake.

Some trials may last for years to strengthen our faith in Jesus.

Some Christians will go through some trials in their marriages.

These trials may last for some years.

Some Christians will go through some trials for being single.

Those trials may last for some years.

Some Christians will go through some trials on their jobs.

Those trials may last for some years.

Some Christians will go through some trials in their churches.

Those trials may last for some years.

Everybody who goes to church is not doing the Lord's will.

Going through some trials for Jesus's name's sake will surely strengthen our love for Him.

Some Christians will go through some trials for being sick.

Those trials may last for some years to strengthen your faith in Jesus.

How Much Longer Will it Be?

How much longer will it be, my Lord and savior Jesus Christ, before You come back again to give me eternal life?

How much longer will it be before I see my deceased loved ones again when You come back to raise them from the grave if they are saved in you?

How much longer will it be before You, oh Lord, close probation on this world after You stand up and say that is it is finished?

How much longer will it be before You, my Lord, change me from mortal to immortal?

How much longer will it be for you to raise me from the grave if I am dead before you come back again on the clouds of glory?

How much longer will it be for the gospel to be preached to every man, woman, boy and girl around the world?

How much longer will it be for You, oh Lord, to remove Your Holy Spirit away from this world for all of your children to be sealed in You?

Some Educated People

Some educated people can be the hardest people to talk to.

Some educated people can be the hardest people to get along with.

Some educated people can be the hardest people to love.

Some educated people can be the hardest people to trust.

Some educated people can be the hardest people to please.

Some educated people can be the hardest people to live with.

The Pharisees and scribes were educated people who tried to make it hard for Jesus Christ to save people's souls.

The religious leaders, priests and elders made it hard for Jesus to minister to people.

They were educated.

Some educated people can be the hardest people to convince to believe in Jesus Christ.

The Joy of Life

The joy of life is that we can learn from our mistakes.

The joy of life is that we can mature more and more.

The joy of life is that we can choose right from wrong.

The joy of life is that we can see.

The joy of life is that we can hear.

The joy of life is that we can smell.

The joy of life is that we can touch.

The joy of life is that we can taste.

The joy of life is that we can reason.

The joy of life is that we can talk.

The joy of life is that we can listen.

The joy of life is that we can walk.

The joy of life is that we can believe in Jesus Christ.

The joy of life is that we can be saved in Jesus Christ.

The joy of life is that we can live to love Jesus and love one another.

We are Created in the Image of God

The sun will shine so beautiful and bright, but the sun is not created in the image of God.

The full, white moon will glow so mysterious all night long, but the moon is not created in the image of God.

The stars will sparkle so bright in outer space, but the stars are not created in the image of God.

The mountains will reach up so high in the sky, but the mountains are not created in the image of God.

Nature will give us its awesome peace and quietness, but nature is not created in the image of God.

The oceans, rivers and seas will flow so majestic with a water surface above the deep bliss, but the oceans, rivers and seas are not created in the image of God.

The sky will open wide and cover over this whole world, but the sky is not created in the image of God.

All the animals will fully understand their own kind, but they are not created in the image of God.

God created every man, woman, boy and girl in his image.

We are most wonderfully made above all nature and above every animal.

We can make choices and can reason like God.

Some People

Someone may ask you if you're doing all right, but his or her body language may tell you that this question is not sincere.

Some people will not mean you good and well in what they say to you. Their motives are not good.

There were some Pharisees, religious leaders and some elders who asked Jesus some questions with the wrong motives in order to trap Him into saying something wrong.

Some people may ask you if you're doing all right, but they don't truly want to see you doing all right.

They would rather see you looking down and complaining, because it gives them something to talk about.

Some people just won't mean you good and well.

They don't want to see you happy and feeling good.

Some people in the church would rather see you making mistakes than be doing anything right, because they don't mean you good and well.

Some people won't like you if they see things going well in your life.

Some people don't like to see you rise above them, especially if they believe that you are not as smart as them.

Many people didn't mean Jesus Christ good and well.

In their eyes, Jesus wasn't good enough to be the Son of God.

If We are Saved in Jesus

If we are saved in Jesus he will represent our case in heaven.

We may be guilty of robbing someone of his or her innocent words that we may believe to be bad.

If we are saved in Jesus he will represent our case in heaven.

We may be guilty of killing someone's name with our bad words that were said behind their back.

If we are saved in Jesus he will represent our case in heaven.

We may be guilty of lying about someone and making him or her look bad.

If we are saved in Jesus he will represent our case in heaven.

We may be guilty of getting revenge when someone did us wrong.

If we are saved in Jesus he will represent our case in heaven.

We may be guilty of being dishonest with someone.

If we are saved in Jesus he will represent our case in heaven.

Jesus will wipe away our sins if we confess and repent unto Him.

We will be innocent of all of our guilt for being saved in Jesus Christ, and can live a renewed life of loving him and our neighbors.

If we are saved in Jesus he will represent our case in heaven.

We are all guilty of our righteousness being like filthy rages before the Lord.

The Good Things that I Do

The good things that I do I want them to glorify Your holy name, my Lord Jesus Christ.

I don't want to glorify my name that has spots and blemishes.

The good things that I do I want them to be all about You, my Lord and savior Jesus Christ.

I don't want them to be all about me, who can make mistakes in my name.

The good things that I do I want them to be about Your business, my Lord Jesus Christ.

I don't want them to be about my business that can go out of business in my name.

The good things that I do I want them to win souls to You, my Lord Jesus Christ.

I don't want them to win souls to me, who has sins to confess and repent of unto You, my Lord.

The good things that I do I want them to draw people to You, my Lord Jesus Christ.

I don't want them to draw people to me, who can pull away from You, my Lord, in ways that I don't see.

The good things that I do I want them to honor Your holy name, my Lord.

I don't want them to honor my name, which has been dishonored through some bad choices that I made.

Like a Canoe Without Its Paddle

A canoe without its paddle will drift away, out to sea.

We are like a canoe without its paddle, drifting out to the sea of selfishness without Jesus Christ in our lives.

Like a canoe without its paddle, our life has no direction and will drift without Jesus in our lives.

We can get in a canoe, but if we don't have any paddles to steer us where we need to go, we will drift out to sea and be lost.

Without Jesus in our hearts, minds, and souls, we will be lost in sin.

Nobody would want to get into a canoe without having paddles to steer the course so we can go where we want to go.

If everybody thinks that way about Jesus steering us on the course of His salvation, no one would want to be lost on the sea of darkness.

Like a canoe without its paddle, you and I are drifting on the sea of this sinful world.

If we don't pick up the paddles of denying self and pick up our cross and follow Jesus Christ on the sea of his amazing grace, we will be lost.

It's Like a Bad Dream

Living in this world of days that we can't put our trust in is like having a bad dream that we cannot wake ourselves from

Living in this world of nights that we can't put our trust in is like having a bad dream that we can't wake ourselves from.

Living in this world of not knowing what will happen next is like having a bad dream that we can't wake ourselves from.

Living in this world of trouble that can come our way at any time is like having a bad dream that we can't wake ourselves from.

Living in this world of many evil deeds looking like they're a good thing is like having a bad dream that we can't wake ourselves from.

Living in this world of selfishness looking like a kind deed is like having a bad dream that we can't wake ourselves from.

Living in this world of prejudice looking so naked is like having a bad dream that we can't wake ourselves from.

Only Jesus Christ can wake us up out of the bad dream when he comes back again to take us out of this sinful world that is like a bad dream.

We will wake up in immortality with our bad dream gone forever as this sinful world passes away.

Some People Will Only Love You

Some people will only love you if you are living in a big, beautiful house.

Some people will only love you if you are driving an expensive car.

Some people will only love you if you are educated.

Some people will only love you if you are beautiful.

Some people will only love you if you are rich.

Some people will only love you if you are handsome.

Some people will only love you if you have a good paying job.

Some people will only love you if you are very talented.

Some people will only love you if you kiss up to them.

Some people will only love you if you are talkative.

Some people will only love you if you let them get away with doing wrong things.

Some people will only love you if you let them control you.

Some people in the church will only love you if you don't step on their toes with the truth of God's word.

Some people in the church will only love you if you are very gifted.

Some people in the church will only love you if you agree with them on every word they say.

Jesus Christ, the Lord, loved you before you were born, when you knew nothing.

The Devil Loves to Tempt Us

The devil loves to tempt us with his good aroma and lovely looking temptations.

The devil loves to tempt us with the delicious taste of his temptations.

The devil's temptations can make us hungry for his food of selfish desires that can taste so good to our souls.

The devil loves to tempt us with his tasteful wines of pride that can intoxicate us and make us believe that we are self-made.

The devil's temptations can seem so good that we won't care about where the Lord brought us from and what the Lord brought us through.

The devil's delicious tasting temptations can cause us to take a back seat and relax while enjoying temporary things.

Jesus loves for us to eat his spiritual food that will give us a front seat to enjoy his spiritual desserts.

The devil loves to tempt us with his delicious desserts of temptation that cause us to put a lot of calories of sin into our lives.

Jesus Christ, our Lord and savior, gave up his life on the cross for our sins and he rose from the grave to help us to resist the devil's temptations of sinful appetizers.

Is it Really Worth It?

Is it really worth it to turn our backs on the Lord and chase behind temporary things that will one day pass away?

Is it really worth it to believe in anything and anyone who is not in line with the bible that teaches us to believe in Jesus Christ?

Is it really worth it to be a friend to this world and want to please this world that can't give us the love, joy, and peace that Jesus Christ, our Lord, can give to us?

Is it really worth it to be proud about our accomplishments and material things we have that give us no eternal life?

Only Jesus Christ can give us eternal life that is for humble souls unto Him.

Is it really worth it to try to work our way into heaven?

That will never please the Lord, who knows that we can't save our own souls.

Is it really worth it to knock people down with our words, when Jesus loves them and wants to save their souls from being lost?

Is it really worth it to give up on people who we believe to be lost?

If we make it to heaven, we might be surprised by who we see there.

We Can Bring Hardship on Ourselves

We can bring hardship on ourselves by doing what we want to do.

If we don't do what the Lord will have us do, we will sooner or later regret it.

We can bring hardship on ourselves by leaning to our own selfish desires that will sooner or later catch up with us and can leave us feeling so empty.

We can bring hardship on ourselves by not doing God's holy will.

God's will for us is to keep His commandments every day.

We can bring hardship on ourselves by putting the blame on someone else for our own mistakes.

We can bring hardship on ourselves by taking things into our own hands and not leaving it in the Lord's hands.

We can bring hardship on ourselves by wanting the glory and praise that belongs to the Lord Jesus Christ.

We can bring hardship on ourselves by not waiting on the Lord.

We can do things our own way and set ourselves back for years.

We can bring hardship on ourselves by not listening to the Holy Spirit, who will always tell us the truth to set us free from being hardheaded.

The Lord Will Bring

The Lord will bring certain people into your life at just the right time to encourage and help you get through tough times.

The Lord will bring certain people into your life at just the right time to help you along your life's journey.

The Lord is not slack in blessing you with certain people at just the right time to give you the push you need.

The Lord Jesus Christ will bring certain people into your life at just the right time to love you and be a good friend to you.

The Lord will bring certain people into your life at just the right time to help you wise up and do better.

The Lord is always on time to bring certain people into your life and my life at just the right time to help us hold onto Him.

The Lord always has a group of certain people to come into our lives at the right time to give us some good advice that we need to do well in life.

Put It Upon Our Hearts

When the Lord puts it upon our hearts to say something we must say it to help someone who needs to hear it.

The Lord will always put upon our hearts to say something true and good to help someone wise up and do His holy will.

When the Lord puts it upon our hearts to do something, we must do it to help someone who is in need.

The Lord will never put upon our hearts something that is too hard for us to do.

The Lord is always on time to inspire us with what to say at the right time.

The Lord is always on time to show us what to do at just the right time.

The Lord will always put it upon our hearts to love and obey Him and to love one another.

Our Lord and savior Jesus Christ will put it upon our hearts to deny self and pick up our crosses and follow him day after day.

We Are Living In

We are living in a world where anything can go wrong at any time of the day and night.

For so very long, up until today, this is not a safe world to live in.

We live in a world where a friend could be an enemy.

We can't keep ourselves safe in this world where it's so easy to make big mistakes that could take us to the graveyard.

Every day, so many people are living large and don't care about cutting their lives short.

Our real, true protection is the Lord, who will always see the danger that we don't see coming our way.

We are living in these last days when the devil knows that his time is very short.

The Lord will give him what he deserves.

We are living in perilous times under the sunshine.

Many people just don't even care to serve the Lord.

It shows and tells in their actions that are not kind.

News Gets Around

News gets around by people telling something new that you and I haven't heard before, and we always want to know something new.

There is always a new story to be told by people.

Wanting to know the news is nothing new in this world.

News spread around about Jesus Christ healing the sick, feeding the hungry, casting out demons and raising the dead.

That news about Jesus traveled fast throughout the region.

That was surely good news for people who wanted to be healed, but it was bad news for the Pharisees and religious leaders.

News gets around quickly, especially bad news. It travels so fast around the world.

Good news is hardly ever told on the daily news shows.

News gets around by people who love to spread some new information just to get attention.

The gospel news about Jesus Christ will spread around the world, where everybody won't be happy to hear and accept it.

The good news is all about Jesus being the Son of God and the light of the world.

In This Life

In this life we will get bored sometimes.

In the eternal life that Jesus wants to give us, we will never get bored. There will always be something to do.

In this life there will be some days that will not be easy to get through.

In the eternal life that Jesus wants to give to us, every day will be easy to get through.

In this life we will get discouraged sometimes.

In the eternal life that Jesus wants to give to us, we will never get discouraged.

In this life we will feel like giving up on our dreams sometimes.

In the eternal life that Jesus wants to give to us, we will never feel like giving up on anything.

In this life we will make some mistakes sometimes.

In the eternal life that Jesus wants to give to us, we will never make any mistakes.

In this life we will be misunderstood sometimes.

In the eternal life that Jesus wants to give to us, we will never be misunderstood.

In this life we will go through some trials sometimes for Jesus' name's sake.

In the eternal life that Jesus wants to give to us, we will never have any trials to go through.

In the eternal life that Jesus wants to give to us, one day, we will be made perfect without sin that is only in this life.

Some People Won't Like You

If you look like you have yourself together, some people won't like you.

You could feel good about yourself and some people won't like you.

They would rather see you feeling down and out.

If you are doing well in your life, some people won't like you.

They would rather see you doing badly.

Some people don't want to see you doing as well as they are.

You are not good enough for them.

Even in the church, some people don't want to see you doing good things in Jesus' holy name.

They would rather see you doing nothing for Jesus.

Some people in church don't want to see you prosper.

They would rather see you begging for food to eat.

They would rather see you begging for money to pay your bills.

Jesus had himself together all the time when he lived here on earth.

Many of those religious leaders and church folks didn't like Jesus for being without sin.

They always tried to trap Jesus into saying something wrong and doing something wrong.

Some church folks wont' like you for giving Jesus Christ your best with the gifts that he gave to you.

You Can Be Smart

You can be smart and not use good judgment.

You can be smart and be selfish.

You can be smart and talk bad.

You can be smart and do wrong things.

You can be smart and make bad choices.

You can be smart and be controlling.

You can be smart and be proud and arrogant.

You can be smart and be corrupt.

You can be smart and make mistakes.

You can be smart and sin against the Lord.

You can be smart and not do what is right.

You can be smart and not use your common sense.

You can be smart and be good.

Being smart is having quick intelligence.

Being smart doesn't make you faultless.

Pass Over

A shadow will pass over the landscape.

A storm will pass over you and me.

The truth will pass over a lie.

Love will pass over hate.

Good will pass over evil.

You and I will pass over self, for denying self and picking up our cross to follow Jesus Christ is the right thing to do.

Jesus has passed over all of our sins to save us.

The sun will pass over the day.

The moon will pass over the night.

Jesus has passed over this life.

Jesus went back to heaven to prepare a place for you and me.

Freedom will pass over slavery.

Jesus has set us free from being a slave to the devil.

Jesus paid the price for our freedom with his life on the cross.

We can choose to not be a slave to anyone, even if it will cause us to lose our lives.

Things Do Come Up

Things do come up and can cause us to change our minds.

Things do come up and can leave us speechless.

Things do come up and can catch us off guard.

Things do come up and can surprise us.

Things do come up and can frighten us.

Things do come up and can put stress on us.

Things do come up and can depress us.

Things do come up and can make us happy.

Things do come up and can make us sad.

Things do come up and can make us laugh.

Things do come up and can encourage us.

Things do come up and can cause us to pray to Jesus.

Things do come up and can cause us to hold on to Jesus.

Things do come up and can cause us to keep our trust in Jesus.

Things do come up and can cause us to keep our hope in Jesus.

In This Present Day

In this present day I am a lot stronger in the Lord.

In this present day I have no desire to do the things I used to do.

In this present day I have no desire to say the words that I used to say.

In this present day I have no desire to think the thoughts I used to think.

I am a lot stronger in my Lord and savior Jesus Christ.

In the past years, I was foolish to want what I couldn't have.

In this present day, Jesus has set me free from the things that weren't good for me to hold onto.

In this present day my eyes are open to a lot more truth of God's holy word.

In this present day I am glad to be stronger in the Lord.

I don't want to ever be weak again by doing my own will.

In this present day I want to live my life being obedient to the Lord.

I don't want to desire anything that's not in the Lord's will.

In this present day I am a lot stronger in the Lord.

What You Went Through

What you went through, O Lord, is a lot more than what I could ever say.

What you went through, O Lord, is a lot more than what I could ever do.

What you went through, O Lord, is a lot more than what I could ever think.

What you went through, O Lord, is a lot more than what I could ever imagine.

What you went through, O Lord, to save me from my sins is a lot more than what I could ever feel.

What you went through, O Lord, is a lot more than what I could ever dream about.

You, my Lord and savior Jesus Christ, lived on earth without ever sinning against God to help me to overcome the sins in my life.

You, my Lord and savior Jesus Christ, gave up Your sinless life on the cross to save me from being lost in my sins.

God is Forever Beyond

God is forever beyond our senses.

God is forever beyond our intelligence.

God is forever beyond our knowledge.

God is forever beyond our wisdom.

God is forever beyond our time.

God is forever beyond our life.

God is forever beyond our days.

God is forever beyond our mind.

God is forever beyond our heart.

God is forever beyond our existence.

God is forever beyond our words.

God is forever beyond you and me.

Have Bible Knowledge

A lot of people have bible knowledge of Jesus Christ, but they don't believe in Jesus Christ.

A lot of people have bible knowledge of Jesus Christ, but they don't obey Jesus Christ.

A lot of people have bible knowledge of Jesus Christ, but they won't give a testimony about Jesus Christ bringing them through their trials.

A lot of people have bible knowledge of Jesus Christ, but they won't pray to Jesus Christ.

A lot of people have bible knowledge of Jesus Christ, but they don't have a relationship with Jesus Christ.

A lot of people have bible knowledge of Jesus Christ, but they won't put their trust in Jesus Christ.

A lot of people have bible knowledge of Jesus Christ, but they don't love Jesus Christ.

Spreading the Gospel

Spreading the gospel of Jesus Christ is not about making a good name for ourselves.

Spreading the gospel of Jesus Christ is not about being popular.

Spreading the gospel of Jesus Christ is not about getting rich.

Spreading the gospel of Jesus Christ is about winning souls to confess and repent of their sins unto Jesus, who can save us from our sins.

We can spread the gospel of Jesus Christ in sermons.

We can spread the gospel of Jesus Christ in gospel songs.

We can spread the gospel of Jesus Christ in testimonies.

We can truly spread the gospel of Jesus Christ in in our renewed Christian Life.

We can spread the gospel of Jesus Christ in by our love for Him and by our love for one another in the church.

What They Want to Hear

If you don't tell people what they want to hear, they won't have much to say to you day after day and year after year.

Many people will not say much to you if you are not talking about what can make them feel good or make their day.

Even in the church, some people won't talk to you and me if we are not important enough. We will be invisible to them.

Jesus Christ didn't tell the Pharisees and religious leaders what they wanted to hear to make them feel good before they laid down to sleep.

Many people love to hear what will make them feel good, even if it's not true. They don't care if they're deceived.

Many people in the church want to hear sermons about certain people who they judge to be messed up.

We are all messed up.

Jesus will always tell us what we need to hear, but we wont' always like it if we are living in our sins.

We Know That

We know that God deserves all the glory and praise.

The Lord doesn't want us to treat one another like it doesn't matter how we treat one another..

We know that God gave us His only begotten Son, Jesus Christ, to save us from our sins.

God doesn't want us to cause one another to sin against Him as if it doesn't matter to us to do that.

We know that God loves us all the same every day.

God doesn't want us to show respect of persons, even though there are people who will choose who they love most.

We know that God created all the angels.

God doesn't want us to be lost like the fallen angels.

When His son, Jesus Christ, comes back again, He will give us immortality to be made like the angels in heaven.

A Quiet Night

A quiet night can surely soothe our minds from the stress that a day can bring on us so unkind.

On a quiet night, we can get a good night's sleep and dream away all night long into the deep unconscious.

On a quiet night, the Lord can speak to us and show us things so crystal clear, like feeling the wind that blows on us.

Jesus went out to pray to His heavenly Father on some quiet nights that were so peaceful to Jesus, who came from heaven and lived a sinless life among sinful men.

People who love to party all night long don't know what it means to enjoy a quiet night out. That may seem so odd to party lovers.

A quiet night can surely slow us down to meditate on the Lord, who can be so patient to wait on us to listen to His Holy Spirit on a quiet night.

A Double Life

I don't want to live a double life.

I want to live right unto my Lord and savior Jesus Christ.

I don't want to have one foot in the church and one foot outside the church. That won't work in the eyes of my Lord.

I want to serve my master, Jesus Christ, each and every day.

I can't serve two masters in any kind of way.

Many church folks are living a double life.

They go to church and pretend to love the Lord, and then when they are not in church their hands are filled with sinning against the Lord.

A double life is for a hypocrite to live, because that's surely not doing God's will.

Many church folks are giving into that temptation that will not fulfill their life with peace.

I don't want to live a double life that will give me no joy, only trouble and strife.

I want to have both feet in the church.

I don't want to be lost in my sins.

I want to make Jesus Christ my choice every day.

The Deep Waters Of

The deep waters of our thoughts can run deep in thinking on the wrong things before we lay down to sleep.

The deep waters of our hearts can run deep in bad feelings that may cause someone's scream to echo through the ceiling.

The deep waters of our life can run deep in living by our own will.

Living by the Lord's can show us why the waters surface is safe to float on.

The deep waters of our souls can run deep in the Lord's salvation to save our souls from being lost in sin.

The deep waters of our destiny can run deep by the choices we make to set our destiny's course to heaven or hell on the seas of our life.

The deep waters of our free will can run deep in a mystery only the Lord will always solve.

Our free will gives us the victory over our own will.

No Matter What Good You Do

No matter what good you do, some people will not be blessed.

It doesn't make them bad to not be blessed.

Bad remarks can hurt but they can help us to do better.

Some people will not be pleased by what you do. That is the way life is.

Some people weren't pleased by what Jesus did when he lived on earth.

Some people weren't blessed by Jesus' perfect ministry work.

No matter what good you and I do, we will get some negative responses.

Jesus had negative responses from the religious leaders.

Some religious people can be your worst critics.

They were Jesus' worst critics too.

No matter what good you do, some people will discourage you.

It's up to you to shake the dust off your feet.

Jesus shook the dust off his feet and moved on beyond criticism.

Everybody May Not

Everybody may not hear a song the same way.

It can sound so different from one person to the next person, day after day.

Everybody may not hear a sermon the same way.

Even though it's about Jesus Christ, like the preacher says.

Everybody may not pray the same way, even though it can still be answered before we lay down to sleep.

Everybody may not be on the same spiritual level in Jesus Christ's holy and precious name.

Everybody in the church may not see eye to eye in spiritual things about Jesus Christ, who we never see.

Everybody in the church may not give Jesus Christ their best in what they do in His name that is not about making us a success in life.

His holy name is about saving our souls from being lost.

You and I Can Give Up on People

You and I can give up on people who we believe won't change.

You and I can write people off because we don't see change in them.

You and I can want to forget about people who are not serving the Lord.

The Lord doesn't give up on anyone.

We can give up on Him being able to change people's hearts so they repent and believe in Him.

If people are not on our spiritual level in the Lord, we can ignore them as if they are not present in our eyesight.

We are not always patient with people when they are slow to turn away from their selfish ways.

We don't want to always wait on people to change and come to our spiritual level.

You and I can give up on people if they don't understand our belief in the Lord.

If Jesus gives up on people, it's because they're six feet under the ground.

The Most Effective Ministry

The most effective ministry is to give kind looks to people.

The most effective ministry is to talk to people right.

The most effective ministry is to act right to people.

The most effective ministry is to treat people right.

The most effective ministry is to show people that you love the Lord Jesus Christ.

The most effective ministry is to show people that you love them.

The most effective ministry is to dress right.

The Lord gives everybody a ministry in the church.

Keeping the Lord's commandments is the most effective ministry in the church and outside the church.

People would rather see you and me living our lives unto our Lord and savior Jesus Christ.

The most effective ministry is to live right by the bible truths that we know to be most effective day after day.

When It's Usually Quiet

When it's usually quiet the Lord can show us things so clear like we can feel the wind that blows.

When it's usually quiet the Lord can help us make the right decisions that we can trust.

When it's usually quiet the Lord can speak to our hearts like we can see the full, white moon and all the stars on a clear night.

When it's usually quiet we can feel the Lord being close to us who should always love Him the most.

When it's usually quiet the Lord can help us to use our good senses so grand.

When it's usually quiet the Lord can fill us with His holy spirit to do His holy will.

When it's usually quiet the Lord can heal us from our broken sins that make us spiritually ill.

It's Done and Over With

What happened in the past is done and over with.

We can't bring it back to change what it did to us, no matter how we dwell on it.

We need to let the past retire from its work to go and be done and over with like a tree that won't grow anymore.

Living in the past won't change what is going on in our lives today.

What truly matters for us is to want to change our ways.

All that happened in the past is done and over with like a dream that passes over us in the night.

If we live in the past, we can't face up to change.

We are living in changing times today that can be strange to anyone who loves to live in the past that is done and over with.

One day, all sin will be done and over with, from the highest mountain cliff to the deepest ocean.

God will destroy all sin and create a new heaven and new earth in his Son, Jesus' name.

You and I won't be done and over with for being saved in Jesus Christ.

The past is a bridge that many people won't cross over in life.

It is not done and over with for them.

We Will Very Often Remember

We will very often remember what we said, whether we are feeling bad about what we said or glad about what we said.

We will very often remember what we have done, whether we meant well or had bad intentions under the sun.

A criminal will very often remember all the crimes he committed, but that's not worth a dime to the judge.

We will very often remember what we said, especially if it's something wrong and we have a conscious that's strong.

We will very often remember that we did something wrong that could stay on our minds until we are long gone to the grave.

We will very often remember many of our sins, if not all of them, but we can repent of them in the winter, spring, summer and fall.

Jesus Christ, our Lord and savior, can cleanse us of all our sins and remember them no more as we live a Christian life upon the land.

Who Can?

Who can love us more than Jesus?

Who can tell us the truth better than Jesus?

Who can help us more than Jesus?

Who can heal us better than Jesus?

Who can encourage us better than Jesus?

Who can motivate us better than Jesus?

Who can educate us better than Jesus?

Who can understand us better than Jesus?

Who can make us happy more than Jesus?

Who can give us strength more than Jesus?

Who can bless more than Jesus?

Who can talk to us better than Jesus?

Who can listen to us more than Jesus?

Who can change our lives for the better more than Jesus?

Who can we live for to be better? The answer is Jesus!

Only Jesus Can Help You Overcome

If lust is your weakness, getting married won't help you to overcome that lust. Only Jesus can help you to overcome that lust.

If pride is your weakness, helping people won't help you to overcome that pride. You can boast about how many people you've helped. Only Jesus can help you to overcome that pride.

If greed is your weakness, giving money to people won't help you to overcome that greed. You might want them to give the money back to you. Only Jesus can help you to overcome that greed.

If backbiting is your weakness, saying a few good words about people won't help you to stop backbiting. Only Jesus can help you to overcome that backbite.

If telling lies is your weakness, telling the truth for one minute won't help you to overcome telling lies. Only Jesus can help you to overcome telling lies.

If committing crimes is your weakness, doing one good thing won't help you to overcome committing crimes. Only Jesus can help you to overcome committing crimes.

Only Jesus can help you and me overcome our weaknesses.

Jesus Lived a Normal Life

When Jesus was a little baby, he probably cried sometimes.

When Jesus was a little boy, he probably played with other little children.

When Jesus was a teenager, he probably went through some changes in life.

Jesus did not let his human desires cause Him to sin against God.

Jesus lived a normal life in obedience unto His parents every day.

Jesus lived a normal life and socialized with other people.

Jesus lived a normal life in caring for the animals.

Jesus was a normal baby who could cry.

Jesus was a normal boy who talked to other boys and girls.

Jesus was a normal man who talked to other men and women.

Jesus was normal without sin.

He never sinned against God in his normal life.

We don't understand what it means to be without sin.

It's like a mystery to us sinners that Jesus lived on earth without ever sinning against God.

Jesus was perfect in every word that he said.

Jesus was perfect in everything that he did.

We don't know what it's like to be without sin.

The brightest and the smartest of people don't know what it is like to be without sin.

Only Jesus Christ, the Son of God, was without sin as he lived a normal life.

The Spiritual Things

The spiritual things from the Lord are the greatest blessings we can receive from Him.

The material things can get old and fade.

The material things can fill us with pride.

The spiritual things are something that we can always hold onto with humility.

The spiritual things will always outlast the material things.

The material things can put stress on us.

The material things are temporary.

The spiritual things are the fruit of the Holy Spirit in our lives.

The spiritual things are the abundance of life.

The material things are only for this life.

Spiritual will go on into eternal life.

The spiritual things can prolong our lives.

Material things can shorten our lives if we love material things more than Jesus.

Jesus Christ, our Lord, loves to bless us with spiritual things the most.

The spiritual things cannot turn us away from the Lord.

Material things can turn us away from the Lord.

Material things can corrupt us.

I Know that I Will Be Blessed

I know that I will be blessed when I walk through the church doors to enter the church that's filled with ministry works.

I know that I will be blessed when I hear the Sabbath school lesson being taught by the Sabbath school teacher giving a good message about Jesus Christ, my Lord and savior.

I know that I will be blessed when I get a hug from my brothers and sisters who will never mug me.

I know that I will be blessed when I hear a children's story being told to the little children who are so much more precious than gold.

I know that I will be blessed when I hear a song that someone sings about my Lord Jesus who will never do me wrong.

I know that I will be blessed when I hear a sermon about my Lord Jesus Christ who I have no reason to ever doubt.

I know that I will be blessed when I see my sisters and brothers worshipping the Lord and loving one another.

I know that I will be blessed for being in the household of faith where I can lay down all of my burdens to Jesus Christ on the holy Sabbath day of rest.

I know that I will be blessed to feel the Holy Spirit beyond words to say.

Jesus Can Fix Broken People

Many people love to fix what is broken.

Many people are good at fixing things that are broken.

It doesn't take a lot to break something into pieces.

We usually know when something is broken.

We just don't know when we will break something.

Whatever is broken surely needs fixing.

We will usually throw away what we can't fix.

We are broken in sin and can't fix ourselves.

Many people will throw themselves away by giving up on hope.

Our only true living hope is Jesus Christ, who can always fix broken people.

You and I are so broken up in sin and only Jesus can fix us.

Many people don't want to be fixed by Jesus because they believe that they can fix themselves.

Broken people can't fix broken people.

Sin has broken us all up to fall short of the glory of God.

When Jesus lived on earth, He never fell short of the glory of God.

Many people are broken in their hearts.

Many people are broken in their relationships.

Jesus can fix anybody who is broken.

We are all broken in sin.

When We Go Through

When we go through some hard times in life, reality will show us that we may pay the total price.

When we go through some hard times in life, deception can surely trick us so we can't withstand the truth that is real and true.

When we go through some hard times in life, it can throw our good common sense off balance and it will show and tell in our decisions.

When we go through some hard times in life, time can seem to move so slow, like the shade moving across the beautiful green grass on the ground.

When we go through some hard times in life, the pressure cannot be measured and our enemies will treasure our pressure.

When we go through some hard times in life, for Jesus' name's sake, some people will put the blame on us like they did with Job who got blamed for the hard times he went through.

Is Ordinary

Life is ordinary for us to live day after day.

The air that we breathe is ordinary.

The ground is ordinary to walk on.

The river will flow into the ocean so ordinary.

Life is ordinary, like the leaves hanging on the trees.

When we lay down to sleep, it's ordinary.

The day and the night are ordinary.

Life, health and strength are ordinary.

It's the ordinary things in life that will truly matter to you and me.

Being ordinary is not enough for people who want to be extraordinary.

Life is ordinary.

We should be happy to be ordinary people.

God can use ordinary people to do some extraordinary things.

Life is ordinary like a bell that rings.

The birds will fly so ordinary when many people strive to be extraordinary.

There are People

There are people who will insult your intelligence to make you look like you don't have good sense to say and do something right.

Those kinds of people can be lethal to your intelligence.

The Pharisees tried to insult Jesus' intelligence by trying to catch him in a lie.

They could never trick Jesus to sin against God.

There are people who are so quick to take what you say in the wrong way when you mean them good and well.

Jesus always meant people good and well, like he would do day after day when he lived on earth without sin.

There are people who will pretend to be your friend and will in a slick way insult your intelligence to make you look small-minded.

Jesus will never insult our intelligence all through our lives.

We can always talk to Jesus, who understands every word that we say.

He would never look down on us and make us look stupid.

The Real True Life

The real true life is eternal life.
Only Jesus Christ can give it to us so very nice.
This life will give us wars.
This life will give us injustice.
This life will give us hatred.
This life will give us grief.
This life will give us heartaches.
This life will give us crimes.
This life will give us disappointments.
This life will give us death.
This life will give us pride.
This life will give us partiality.
This life will give us immorality.
This life will give us jealousy.
This life will give us prejudice.
This life will give us poverty.
This life will give us greed.
This life will give us lies.
This life will give us corruption.
This life will give us failures.
The real true life is eternal life that is a perfect life without sin.
This life will give us sin.

Many people are living their lives like they're living in heaven on earth.

The real true life will give us heaven in the end.

This life will give us temporary things that will one day pass away.

This life will give us sickness.

This life will give us rebellion against God.

You

You can't make yourself great.

It will take millions of people to make you great.

You can't make yourself rich.

It will take millions of people to make you rich.

You can't make yourself famous.

It will take millions of people to make you famous.

You will know that you are gifted if people tell you that you are gifted.

You will know that you are talented if people tell you that you are talented.

You are saved in the Lord Jesus Christ if you believe in Him and are baptized.

People will know if you love them if you treat them right.

Jesus Christ knows you love Him, if you keep his commandments.

You will know if you love yourself, if you treat yourself right.

You will know who you are if you are honest with yourself.

You will know Jesus Christ if you have a relationship with Him.

You will know Jesus Christ if you study the bible.

Only Jesus Christ is better than you.

He knew you in your mother's womb.

Jesus knows you better than you know yourself.

God Created Us to Love

God created us to love Him first, above all others.

God created us to love one another.

This world still exists because of God's love.

There would be no families if there was no love.

There would be no friends if there was no love.

Every human being would be fighting and killing one another if there was no love.

The human race would destroy life here on earth if there was no love.

God created us to love even though everybody will not love God.

God created us to love even though everybody will not love one another.

God showed us His love for us when He gave His only begotten Son to die for our sins and rise from the grave to save us from our sins.

There is no love in abusing people and killing people.

There is no love in using people and taking away what they possess.

God created us to love and not hate.

Jesus Christ, our Lord and savior, is the highest love of God.

If we don't love Jesus, we don't love God.

Everybody Will Answer to God

Everybody will answer to God for every good thought.

Everybody will answer to God for every bad thought.

Everybody will answer to God for every good word.

Everybody will answer to God for every bad word.

Everybody will answer to God for every bad motive.

Everybody will answer to God for every good intent.

Everybody will answer to God for every good deed.

Everybody will answer to God for every bad deed.

Everybody will answer to God, great and small.

Everybody will answer to God, rich, upper middle class, middle class and poor.

Everybody will answer to God during one's judgment hour that will come.

Everybody who is alive and everybody who has ever lived will answer to God.

Jesus Christ is with God.

He knows everybody's answers.

Do We Ever Trespass on God's Holy Ground?

Do we ever trespass on God's holy ground? We do if we walk on God's holy ground holding grudges.

Do we ever trespass on God's holy ground? We do if we walk on God's holy ground with sexual immorality.

Do we ever trespass on God's holy ground? We do if we walk on God's holy ground trying to make ourselves look good.

Do we ever trespass on God's holy ground? We do if we walk on God's holy ground with jealousy in our hearts.

Do we ever trespass on God's holy ground? We do if we walk on God's holy ground with gossip and backbiting.

Do we ever trespass on God's holy ground? We do if we walk on God's holy ground telling lies.

Do we ever trespass on God's holy ground? We do if we walk on God's holy ground not truly believing in his Son, Jesus Christ.

Do we ever trespass on God's holy ground? We do if we walk on God's holy ground believing that our work will give us favor with God.

Everybody Has a Sin Defect

Everybody has a sin defect to say something wrong.

Everybody has a sin defect to do something wrong.

Everybody has a sin defect to make a bad choice.

Everybody has a sin defect to sin against the Lord.

Everybody has a sin defect to confess and repent unto the Lord, Jesus Christ.

Everybody has a sin defect to fall short of the glory of God.

Everybody has a sin defect to die.

Everybody has a sin defect to live some kind of lie.

Everybody has a sin defect to not trust the Lord in some kind of way.

Everybody has a sin defect to deny self and pick up one's cross and follow Jesus Christ.

Everybody has a sin defect to be lost in sin.

Everybody has a sin defect to pray to Jesus Christ and ask him to forgive us of our sins and save us from our sins.

My Soul Cries Out

My soul cries out unto You, my Lord, for your love that no other love can ever outdo.

My soul cries out unto You, my Lord, for Your mercy that is made new for me every day.

My soul cries out unto You, my Lord, for Your grace that I can never earn to be saved in you.

My soul cries out unto You, my Lord, for Your forgiveness that I don't deserve to be lost in my sins.

My soul cries out unto You, my Lord, for Your righteousness that will make me right with God.

My righteousness is like filthy rags.

You are my Lord and Savior, Jesus Christ, who my soul can cry out unto so far beyond the stars.

Our Human Nature Knows

Nature knows no pride.

Our human nature knows pride.

Nature knows no prejudice.

Our human nature knows prejudice.

Nature knows no jealousy.

Our human nature knows jealousy.

Nature is always so pure and innocent every day, and we can come to nature to put our minds at ease.

Nature knows no lies and no strife.

Our human nature knows lies and strife.

Nature knows no evil.

Our human nature knows evil.

Nature knows no selfishness.

Our human nature knows selfishness.

Because it is human nature to fall into sin, God gave us His only begotten Son to save us from our sins.

God dwells in nature.

God doesn't dwell in our sinful human nature.

There are Many Brilliant People

There are many brilliant people who will twist up lies to make them seem like truth.

In many people's eyes, the truth then becomes a lie.

That fallen angel, Lucifer, twisted his lies and made them seem like truth before many angels who enlisted in his schemes and lies to cause God to look bad.

The devil is using many people who are trying to cause God to look bad by saying that there is no God.

That is not true.

The atheist is at the center of all lies, no matter how brilliant they are.

Many brilliant people love to tell lies and say that it's the truth.

There is no truth in the devil, who is the original liar.

The devil is more brilliant than any human being that he wants to use to tell his lies. They, especially, will believe his lies.

There are many brilliant people who hate to hear the truth and hate to live the truth.

God's truth will never make a mistake and will set us free from the devil's lies.

The Truth Will Judge You

The truth will judge you. You can't fool the truth.

The truth will judge you. You can't deceive the truth.

The truth will judge you. You can't lie to the truth.

The truth will judge you. You can't get rid of the truth.

The truth will judge you. You can't outsmart the truth.

The truth will judge you. You can't run away from the truth.

The truth will judge you. You can't erase the truth.

The truth will judge you. You can't defeat the truth.

The truth will judge you. You can't hide from the truth.

The truth will judge you. You can't bury the truth.

The truth will judge you. You can't charm the truth.

The truth will judge you because Jesus Christ is the living truth.

Jesus will judge our hearts to see if we love Him or not.

You and I are not the truth and cannot judge one another's love for the Lord Jesus Christ.

Who Are We?

Who are we to try to keep someone alive if the Lord says that it's their time to go to the grave?

Who are we to say that this or that will happen if the Lord doesn't allow it to happen?

Who are we to follow through on what we do if the Lord doesn't approve of it?

Who are we to reason things to be right if they don't make any good sense to the Lord?

Who are we to climb up the ladder of success if the Lord doesn't open that door for us?

Who are we to get to where we are going if the Lord doesn't allow us to make it there?

Who are we to get away with doing something evil when the Lord will keep a record of it?

Who are we to live throughout this day if the Lord allows death to chew us up and swallow us down into its belly?

You are Cleansing Me from my Sins

O Lord, you are cleansing me from my sins.

I don't want to do those sinful things that I used to do.

O Lord, you are cleansing me from my sins.

I have no desire to do those sinful things that I used to do.

O Lord, you are cleansing me from my sins.

I don't do many of those sinful things that I used to do.

I confess my sins and I repent of my sins unto You, my Lord and savior Jesus Christ.

You shed your precious blood on the cross to cleanse me from my sins and to save me from my sins.

I am very aware of my seen sins. I want You, my Lord, to cleanse me of these because I want to be saved in You, my Lord.

You will show me my unseen sins that I want to repent of unto You.

O Lord, I don't want to sin against You in words and in what I do, even though I am not without sin.

You are cleansing me from my sins, O Lord, because of my confessions and repentance unto You.

I don't want to deliberately sin against You.

We Can Never Get Lost in Jesus

We can walk through a forest and get lost.

We can drive down a road and get lost.

We can shop in a mall and get lost.

We can never get lost in Jesus Christ.

Our destination is heaven for sure in Jesus.

We can get lost in a big city.

We can get lost out in the country.

We can get lost in the ocean.

We can always know where we are going in Jesus.

The bible tells us so.

We can get lost in the subway.

We can get lost in the dessert.

We can get lost on a cruise ship.

We can always know where we are going in Jesus.

Every day, Jesus will lead us to do His holy will.

We can get lost in our will that only Jesus can find.

Can We Truly Accept?

Can we truly accept everyone for being who they are?

Can we truly accept a serial killer for being who he is?

Can we truly accept a rapist for being who he is?

Can we truly accept a child molester for being who he is?

Can we truly accept people who are evil?

We know that we can accept people who are good.

God loves everyone, but God cannot accept our sins.

We can love everyone, but we can't accept their evil ways.

If you are a good person, you wouldn't accept someone who is evil being who they are.

God loves every soul and wants to save them.

God hates our sins, and won't accept them.

Can we truly accept everyone for being who they are?

Jesus didn't accept the Pharisees for being who they were.

We need to be careful about accepting everyone for being who they are.

Many people are so wicked and that is exactly who they are.

Every true Christian wouldn't accept that.

Surely neither would God.

Will Stand Still

The day will stand still all day long.

You and I will move around here and there.

The night will stand still all night long.

You and I will fall asleep and move around here and there in our dreams.

The sky will stand still way up high above the ground.

You and I will move around here and there on the ground.

The ground will very often stand still and have no earthquakes.

You and I will move around here and there and sometimes go nowhere.

God's salvation will stand still for you and me to be saved in his Son, Jesus Christ.

You and I will move around here and there and can have no repentance in our lives.

Many People Believe in Themselves

Many people believe in themselves to live only by what they see.

They don't believe in Jesus Christ.

Many people believe in themselves to do their own thing all through their lives.

They do not believe in Jesus Christ.

Many people believe in themselves even in the church where sin still exists.

Many people believe in themselves and the words they say.

They don't believe in Jesus Christ, no matter where they live.

Many people believe in themselves, no matter how long they've been going to church.

They don't see anything wrong in not believing in Jesus Christ, who has long gone back to heaven.

Many people believe in themselves to be all-powerful and do all things.

They reject Jesus' holy call for them to believe in Him who owns the great and small.

When We Go to Heaven

When we go to heaven, we will never age or get old.

We will stay young forever and ever from our heads to our toes.

When we go to heaven, we will never get tired or need sleep.

We will stay awake forever and ever to always be up on our feet.

When we go to heaven, we will never feel any pain.

We will feel good forever and ever all of us the same.

When we go to heaven, we will never get sick.

We will stay well forever and ever to show and tell in our eternal life so well.

When we go to heaven, we will be without sin forever and ever and our lives will have no end.

When we go to heaven, we will live forever and ever and never die throughout heaven's eternal land.

When we go to heaven, we will go to heaven with Jesus Christ when he comes back again to give us eternal life.

We can't get to heaven without Jesus taking us there.

We must be saved in Jesus to go to heaven where the angels are everywhere.

Another Day

Another day can seem so far away when we need to do something right away.

Another day can seem so far away from you and me who need to get something done today to be a good thing to see.

Another day may not come our way.

It's the Lord who gives us another day to live.

Another day can seem so far away in our will that is so far beneath God's holy will that give us another day, no matter where we live.

Another day can seem so far away like trying to walk a thousand miles on a long hike across the country.

Only Jesus can give us another day to do what we need to do beyond the dust of the earth.

We can only trust Jesus to give us another day.

Knows Its Place

The sun knows its place to shine down on you and me all day long, that we will surely see.

The moon knows its place to glow down on you and me all night long, that the moon will surely do.

The stars know their place to sparkly down on you and me all night long.

The sky knows its place to hover over you and me whether we are drunk or sober.

The clouds know their place to move across the sky over you and me. We can see it with our own eyes.

The air knows its place for you and me to breathe day in and day out. The air is a great thing that we need.

You and I need to always know our places every day.

Our place is to love and obey Jesus Christ like the bible says.

God gives us all a place to be saved in his Son, Jesus Christ, who knows his place is to give us eternal life.

The Weather of Life

Life can bring us a warm day of things going good for us all day long.

Life can bring us a cool day of disappointment that we can't trust to go away before the day is over.

The weather of life is for only the Lord to predict what that day will bring to us.

The Lord allows this beyond our list of things to do.

Life can bring us a hot day of trouble that we don't see coming our way.

The Lord can protect us and set us free from trouble.

Life can bring us a cold day of grief that can leave us in a state of shock, whether we believe in Jesus Christ or not.

The weather of life has caused Jesus to weep.

Jesus was victorious over the weather of life and made it a stool under his feet.

Someone Asked Me

Someone asked me, "Do you have the holy ghost?"

I said, "Yes, because I believe in Jesus Christ, who is the most positive influence in my life from day to day."

I must believe in Jesus to have the Holy Ghost as I pray to Jesus to give me His holy ghost.

The Holy Ghost teaches me the truth about Jesus, who I can always boast about because He is worthy of all the glory and praise.

If anyone believes in Jesus Christ, they have the Holy Ghost who testifies of Jesus Christ in His holy word.

His word is all truth to set us free from lies in this life.

You and I can't have the Holy Ghost if we don't believe in Jesus Christ, who is God's only begotten Son.

He relieved us from being lost in our sins.

Jesus can save us from our sins and fill us with His holy ghost for believing in him.

He sent the Holy Ghost to this world after He left it and went back to heaven to be with God.

Someone asked me, "Do you have the Holy Ghost?"

I said, "Yes, I do," and I felt so free.

Love is the Greatest Gift

God says that love is the greatest gift because love is very powerful.

Love can lift up our brothers and sisters in the household of faith.

Love is always so very great to mend broken hearts and encourage people to give their life to the Lord.

A gang leader will only pretend to show some love to recruit young people to join his gang.

Even pretend love can be powerful if you and I believe it's true love.

The greatest gift in the church is love. It's above all other gifts.

No gift can have a good effect on people without love.

Love is the past, present and future way.

We can never get enough love.

Love is what we need the most to survive from day to day.

We can have much knowledge of the truth of God's word that says for us to love one another in order to be Disciples of Christ.

Having knowledge without love is so destructive to life.

The Lord is Still Working with Me

The Lord is still working with me, who is not always easy to work with and can sometimes be a pain in the neck for the Lord.

The Lord is still working with me, and the Lord Jesus Christ shows me that he is working things out in my life.

The Lord is still working with me, regardless of me not always trusting Him to show me what I need to see in my life to draw closer to Him.

The Lord is still working with me, who has a slim chance of making it to heaven because I don't always love and obey Him with my whole heart.

The Lord is still working with me, who is a winner who He wants to save in His amazing grace.

The Lord is still working with me, who doesn't know what a day will bring me when the Lord knows before I can say one word.

The Lord is still working with me, and will continue to do so until I go to the grave.

I hope to be saved in Jesus before I go to the grave and sleep away to one day awake and see Jesus on the clouds of glory.

The Combination to Life

The combination to life is our Lord and savior Jesus Christ.

Jesus can always unlock the safe of our hearts so nice.

He knows how to lock up our souls' salvation for being saved in Him.

Jesus puts the fruit of His spirit in the safe of our hearts for us to live a renewed life unto Him every day.

Jesus is the combination to life for you and me to live our lives doing His holy will.

Everyone can know the combination so real for believing in Jesus Christ, who truly fills our safe with His amazing grace.

You and I can celebrate life victories because Jesus rose from the grave to be treasured in the safe of our hearts for holy angels to embrace.

Jesus always knows how to lock up and unlock the mysteries of our lives that the devil can't control around the clock.

If we are living our lives unto Jesus Christ, the combination to life will open up a peace of mind and not strife.

The devil can't steal our combination to life.

There is No Time in Eternity

There is no time in eternity that is all present beyond this world.

The great and the small in this world live on time that is short.

Eternity is forever and ever to always exhort because Jesus is eternal and time has no power over him.

There is no time in eternity beyond the sunshine where eternity is all-present with no trace of time.

Time doesn't exist in outer space below the heaven on high where God lives on his eternal holy throne.

God gives time to fallen, sinful creatures who need time to confess and repent of our sins.

Jesus is eternal for you and me to believe in Him and put our trust in Him to save us from our sins before we bite the dust.

There is no time in eternity that is forevermore real than time that we mortal creatures can't afford to take for granted.

Eternity has no time before the Lord.

The Lord's Yes and No

If the Lord says yes, who can say no, no matter who we are and where we go?

If the Lord says no, who can say yes from the north and south and east and west?

The Lord's yes and no is forever holy and divine beyond our yes and no that is not right all the time.

The Lord's yes can surely bless us from dawn 'til dusk.

The Lord's no can surely bless us to give Him all of our trust.

If the Lord says yes, who are we to say no as if we can make the wind blow?

If the Lord says no, who are we to say yes as if we can pass every test with all A's?

The Lord's yes and no can surely change our lives for the better of being saved in Him, our Lord and savior Jesus Christ.

A Righteous Nation

Nations are built by telling people what to do and not do.

Nations are built by people coming together.

Nations are built by working people.

A righteous nation will believe in Jesus Christ.

A righteous nation will love their neighbors.

A righteous nation will keep peace with other nations.

Nations are built by populating the land.

A righteous nation won't harm its people.

A righteous nation won't kill its people.

Nations are built by winning wars.

A righteous nation will protect its people.

A righteous nation gives freedom to its people.

A righteous nation gives justice to its people.

A righteous nation will keep God's commandments.

God Loves Everybody

God loves everybody, but everybody doesn't love God.

Lucifer and one third of the angels in heaven stopped loving God and fell from heaven.

God's son, Jesus Christ, gave up his life and rose from the grave to save everybody, but everybody will not be saved.

Everybody will not believe in Jesus Christ no matter how much you and I minister to people about Jesus.

God loves everybody, but everybody won't deny self and pick up their cross to follow his son, Jesus.

Everybody will not accept the gospel of Jesus Christ, who loves everybody.

Jesus is God the Son in the fullness of God as well as the Holy Spirit in the trinity Godhead who loves everybody.

Everybody can choose to love God, but that won't happen.

Lucifer was a perfect angel and he stopped loving God.

Lucifer believed that God wasn't good enough to be his God anymore.

Motivate

Nobody in this world can motivate you and me better than the Lord Jesus Christ.

Nobody in this world can motivate you and me more than the Lord Jesus Christ.

The Lord's motivation will make us follow through on the good things that we do.

The Lord's motivation will cause us to feel so good about the good things that we do in His holy name.

Nobody in this world can motivate us like the Lord.

The Lord's motivation will always energize us to be happy about doing what we need to do.

Nobody in this world can motivate us better than the Lord, who will put good words on our tongues to be a blessing to one another.

Motivation from the Lord Jesus Christ will give anyone real, true satisfaction all the time.

Many People Believe

Many people believe that we Christians are weak-minded for believing in Jesus Christ.

They believe that we Christians are a bunch of dreamers who make things up.

Many people believe that we Christians are troublemakers trying to disturb their lives by what we believe.

Many people believe that what's in this world is all that they can get.

We Christians believe that there is a true, living God beyond and above this world.

Many people believe that this world is all that they have to live for day after day.

They have no spiritual life to believe in Jesus Christ who created all things.

Many people believe that we Christians are a bunch of people who believe in a fairy tale.

They believe that the bible is a fairy tale book.

They believe that truth is what they see in this world.

Jesus Christ is the truth that the bible reveals to us.

Many people believe that Jesus is a fairy tale.

We Christians believe that Jesus is real in our lives.

Being a Good Person

Being a good person will not save us from our sins.

Believing in Jesus Christ will save us from our sins.

Being a good person won't get us to heaven.

Only Jesus can get us to heaven.

Being a good person is not enough to make us righteous.

Only through the righteousness of Jesus Christ are we all made to be righteous.

Being a good person won't cleanse us of our sins.

Only Jesus can cleanse us of our sins.

Being a good person won't make us be without sin.

We need to confess and repent of our sins unto Jesus Christ, who is without sin and good all the time.

Being a good person is through the goodness of God, which leads us to repentance.

Bad people will despise good people.

There are No Shortcuts in Life

There are no shortcuts in life.

What we do in life is what we will get in life.

Life won't give us more than what we put into it.

Life has its limits and you and I can't take shortcuts in life.

Jesus Christ, our Lord, didn't take any shortcuts to save us from our sins.

We will reap what we sow and it will catch up with us sooner or later, whether it's good or bad.

Jesus knew that there were no shortcuts to take to not die on the cross for our sins.

Whatever we say will affect people in one way or another.

There are no shortcuts in life for what we say and do.

Our lives will tell the truth on us.

There are no shortcuts to get around the truth.

Human Beings Will Usually

Human beings will usually have a problem with love.

You and I can love a dog and that dog will love us back.

You and I can love a human being who may not love us back.

Human beings are better than an animal, so why do so many human beings have a problem with love?

God created us human beings to love one another.

Animals don't usually have a problem with loving you and me if we love them.

A dog will love us to the end, if we love our dog.

A human being may not love you and me to the end of our lives, no matter how much we love them.

Human beings will usually have a problem with love because of being selfish, which comes from sin.

An animal will treat us right if we treat that animal right.

You can treat a human being right and not get treated right in return.

Human beings will usually have a problem with love.

We are created better than the animals that can love us.

In the Books of History

So many good things that happen in this world are not written down in the books of history.

So many bad things that happen in this world are not written down in the books of history.

There were many people who did good things way back in history, but it was not written down in any book.

We can go back to the bible history that doesn't reveal to us about all the good things that Jesus did when he lived on earth without sin in his flesh.

There will never be enough books to cover everything that happened way back in history.

We will never know everything that happened in this world.

There were many good people who lived a long time ago.

They did many good things that were not written in the books of history.

Only the Lord God knows all the good and bad things that were not written down in the books of history.

We are missing out on the complete history that the Lord truly knows about.

There is No Former Life

There is no former life to live in this world.

There is only one life to live in this world.

Many people believe that they have lived a former life that caused their life today to be a handicap to live.

We only have one physical birth and only one physical life to live in this world.

There is an afterlife to live forever and ever if we are saved in Jesus Christ.

There is no former you and me to ever exist in this world.

God created only one of you and me and not two or three of any of us.

Only one of you and me is enough to live in this sinful world.

There is no former life to live for any human being.

There is another birth that is a spiritual birth to be born again in the Holy Spirit of God for believing in Jesus Christ.

Only Jesus lived a former eternal life before he was born into this sinful world.

No one else has lived a former life.

What Will Jesus Write in the Dust?

What will Jesus write in the dust of our life?

Will he write that we are guilty of not trusting him enough?

What will Jesus write in the dust of our life?

Will he write that we are guilty of doing our own will?

The woman was caught in adultery and brought to Jesus by her accusers.

They wanted to see what Jesus would say and do before them.

They wanted to tempt Jesus into doing something wrong.

Jesus knew that they were doing something wrong to try to trap him.

Jesus must have stooped down and written their sins in the dust with his finger.

What will Jesus write in the dust of our life?

Will he write that we are guilty of judging others who we don't know?

Will Jesus write that we are guilty of putting our trust in this fallen sinful world?

What will Jesus write in the dust of our life?

Will Jesus write that we are guilty of believing that our good works will save us to make it to heaven?

Only Jesus can save us.

In the Courtroom of Time

In the courtroom of time, time is the judge that will give us the trial of our lives.

Time is short in this world.

In the courtroom of time, time is the jury that will give us our verdict.

Our time can run out whether we're young, middle aged or old.

In the courtroom of time, we will be guilty or not guilty of giving god our time in prayer unto him and worshipping him in our home and in the church.

In the courtroom of time, time is our eyewitness, seeing how we live our lives day after day and whether we live it unto the Lord or live it unto the world where time has its limit on us.

In the courtroom of time, time is our defense lawyer, asking God to give us some borrowed time to live and be saved in Jesus Christ.

In the courtroom of time, time is the prosecutor against anyone whose time has run out to be saved and will be lost in the grave.

www.ingramcontent.com/pod-product-compliance
Lightning Source LLC
Chambersburg PA
CBHW052150110526
44591CB00012B/1929